The World Is in Danger

☐ ecological pollution   ☐ food shortages
☐ nuclear war   ☐ population explosion

The author says, "If Christ does not return to the world before long, there will be no world to return to.

"But the world is not going to end in any of these woeful ways. The Lord Jesus is coming, and all these gloomy forecasts do is to highlight the imminence of His return."

God is aware of our situation and has a plan for this planet. This book will tell you all about that plan.

Ian Macpherson

God's Plan For This Planet

GOSPEL PUBLISHING HOUSE
SPRINGFIELD, MISSOURI

02-0517

© 1977 by the Gospel Publishing House
Springfield, Missouri 65802
The chapters in this book were previously published in the
Pentecostal Evangel, © 1975 by the Assemblies of God,
Springfield, Missouri 65802.
Printed in the United States of America
Library of Congress Catalog Card Number: 76-51001
International Standard Book Number: 0-88243-517-5

Contents

CHAPTER 1

God Has a Plan

SOME CHRISTIAN teaching seems to imply that God has no plan for this planet. According to it, His sole concern is to rescue as many souls as possible from this wreck of a world and transport them into the unseen, leaving to a nameless fate this "wandering island in the sky."

These people do not credit God with the slightest interest in the future of the earth. As far as He is concerned, they conclude it is a complete write-off.

But is this so? By no means!

The Bible tells us that God cares tremendously about the fate of this world; He is far from indifferent to its destiny.

True, Scripture does speak of the dissolution of existing material order. There is a terrific passage in 2 Peter where this is graphically depicted in terms reminiscent of nuclear explosions: "The heavens shall pass away with a great noise, and the elements shall melt with fervent heat, the earth also and the works that are therein shall be burned up. . . . The heavens being on fire shall be dissolved" (3:10, 12).

Yes, there is certainly a Biblical warrant for Shakespeare's vast vision of a vanishing world:

The cloud-capped towers, the gorgeous palaces,
The solemn temples, the great globe itself,

Yea, all which it inherit, shall dissolve
And, like this insubstantial pageant faded,
Leave not a rack behind.

God's Plan

Before this takes place, however, God has prodigious plans for this planet. In His prophetic program, events of momentous consequence are scheduled to occur:

The Lord Jesus is to come back personally for His church; there is to be a resurrection of the Christian dead and a transformation of the living Christians before their "gathering together unto him" (2 Thessalonians 2:1; see 1 Thessalonians 4:13-18).

The Antichrist is to be revealed—a scintillating but sinister personality, the Man of Sin in whom the sin of man will be incarnate.

The Jews are to pass through the terrible "time of Jacob's trouble" (Jeremiah 30:7).

Huge power blocs are to emerge in Russia and her satellites, in the Western confederacy, in an alliance of European powers foreshadowed by the Common Market, in Africa, and in the Far East. And all these will converge on Israel where Armageddon, the greatest world war of all time, will be fought.

Then Christ will return with the armies of the sky to destroy His enemies, to be accepted by the Jews as their Messiah, to judge the living nations, and to set up His millennial kingdom during which the devil will be bound.

At the end of the thousand years of Christ's earthly reign, a revolt will flare up but will be quickly quelled. Then the "rest of the dead" will be raised and arraigned before the Great White Throne.

That in barest outline is the Biblical prophetic

program designed for fulfillment prior to the demolition of the existing material order.

A Cosmic Concern

But after "the removal of all things which can be shaken," God will still have a cosmic concern. "And I saw a new heaven and a new earth: for the first heaven and the first earth were passed away.... And I ... saw the holy city, new Jerusalem, coming down from God out of heaven" (Revelation 21:1, 2).

Beyond the turbid times in which he lived, the Apostle was enabled by the Spirit to look on to the Wonderful End. More and more in these days thinking people feel the need of such a vision of the ultimate. For, after all, if when peering into the future what you see is the earth as a lifeless orb, covered with a leprosy of snow, rolling uninhabited through empty space, any present happiness you have is bound to be pretty hollow. Nothing can satisfy the human soul but the sure prospect of final justice and joy in the universe.

And that is what Christianity alone can offer. As Elvet Lewis said: "The God of Jesus Christ can do no wrong. The eternity when time is over will be as stainless as the eternity before time began."

The Sequence

By a happy coincidence each of the major happenings in the panorama of Biblical prophecy can be indicated by a word beginning with the letter R. This alliteration is a great aid in visualizing and memorizing the sequence of events. The R's are as follows:

Rapture (the *Parousia*
Revolution (the Great Tribulation)
Revelation (the *Epiphaneia*)
Realm (the Millennium)

9

Resurrection (the general rising from the dead)

Retribution (the final assize)

Removal (the destruction of the present scheme of things)

Restoration (the establishment of the new heaven and the new earth)

This may be termed the octave of prophetic revelation. It is a panoramic picture of times unborn.

That picture is about to become a *moving* picture. Prophecy is at the point of turning into living history. Things spoken of by ancient seers are soon to be witnessed by modern "see-ers."

"The time is at hand" (Revelation 1:3).

"The day [is] approaching" (Hebrews 10:25).

"The coming of the Lord draweth nigh" (James 5:8).

Fewer than 25 years lie between us and the close of a millennium. The year 2000 will soon be here. "Upon [us] the ends of the world are come" (1 Corinthians 10:11).

For us the Last Things ought, therefore, to be the first things. No branch of Biblical study ought to evoke in us a more intense and intelligent interest—or prove more regulative of our character and conduct. "Seeing then that all these things shall be dissolved, what manner of persons ought [we] to be in all holy conversation and godliness, looking for and hasting unto the coming of the day of God" (2 Peter 3:11, 12).

Man has many ambitious projects on hand today. If these materialize, they may have colossal consequences for the world.

Far more important, however, is the fact that, whether with human cooperation or in spite of opposition, the Almighty is bringing to pass His purposes. "A man's heart may be full of schemes, but the Lord's purpose will prevail" (Proverbs 19:21, NEB).

In the ringing words of Arthur Campbell Ainger:

God is working His purpose out
*   As year succeeds to year;*
God is working His purpose out,
*   And the time is drawing near:*
Nearer and nearer draws the time,
*   The time that shall surely be,*
When earth shall be filled with the glory of God
*   As the waters cover the sea.*

God *has* a plan for this planet—and He will bring it to pass.

CHAPTER 2

Is Jesus Really Coming Back?

D URING World War II the Allies had just won a resounding victory in Europe. The editor of a small newspaper in the Midwest, wanting to give the report the widest possible publicity, instructed his printer to splash it on the front page.

In due course the printer presented a proof bearing a banner headline which seemed designed for the blind.

The editor wasn't satisfied. "Is that the largest type you've got?" he demanded.

"Well," admitted the printer half apologetically, "I do have one size larger, but I was saving that for the Second Coming!"

But is Christ coming back? May we reasonably expect Him to reenter history and assume the leading role in world affairs? Does He, after a lapse of almost 2,000 years, intend to return as literally as does an astronaut who has been to the moon?

If He really is coming back, it will be the greatest newsstory ever.

When Ronald Allison, a British Broadcasting Corporation newsman and journalist, was asked in a television interview what item of news he would most wish to broadcast to the world, he unhesitatingly replied, "The news of the second coming of Christ!"

What an electrifying announcement that will be! For nobody but Jesus is able to tackle the titanic tasks of a world ruler today; nobody but He is competent to unravel the tangled skein of human affairs; nobody but He is big enough to grapple with the great and growing problems now clamoring for solution.

And if He is not coming back to assume such responsibilities, then there is no hope for humanity.

George Bernard Shaw, who will certainly not be suspected of any special leanings toward the Second Coming, felt compelled to confess: "I am ready to admit that, after contemplating the world and human nature for nearly 60 years, I see no way out of the world's misery but the way which would have been found by Christ's will if He had undertaken the work of a modern practical statesman."

That is precisely what Christ purposes to be! It is His role to rule, not only in heaven, but on earth.

Publicly to proclaim that striking hour will be to make the greatest statement in the history of newscasting.

But is He really coming back?

In all honesty there is no precedent for it. Nobody in his right mind looks for a similar reappearance by any other great personality of the past. They are all dead and gone.

After the assassination of Gandhi, a group of his followers assembled to pray. For a while their devotions proceeded quietly enough. But all at once someone broke out: "Come back, Mahatma! Come back! You've been dead 3 days. Come back!"

But Gandhi didn't return. The dead never do.

What rational grounds have we for assuming and asserting that to this universal rule a single exception will be made in favor of Jesus Christ? We have

13

numerous solid bases for believing that He will. Let me mention just two of them here:

First, we believe that Jesus will come back to the earth because He himself expected to do so and forecast that He would.

On that score there cannot be the slightest doubt. As William Neil states in the introduction to his commentary on Thessalonians: "It is impossible to escape the conclusion that the initial impetus to the Church's belief in the return of Christ was given by our Lord himself."

Second, we believe that Christ will come back in the future because He has already come back in the past. His resurrection is presumptive proof of His return. He who came from the *clods* will come from the *clouds*.

The amazing thing is that so few professing Christians today cherish what Titus 2:13 calls that "blessed [literally, happy] hope" at all. Surely if there is even the remotest possibility that the Rapture will happen, the prospect ought to thrill with holy joy the heart of every follower of Jesus!

But no! Many modern Christians give the impression of being embarrassed by the bare mention of it and would almost rather exclude it from their creeds.

Nothing, then, at this juncture in Christian history could exceed in practical importance the inquiry: Is Jesus Christ really coming back to earth?

You will find four broad answers to this question.

It Is a Mistake

One of these answers claims that the Advent expectation was, from the first, a mistake.

There are those who do not hesitate to charge even our Lord Jesus himself with error. They allege that, under the influence of current Jewish apocalyptic ideas,

Jesus sincerely believed that, after His departure from the world, He would return to His disciples; but He was wrong.

Here is what some of these people teach:

"The hope that Christ will reappear in physical manifestation," declares John Mayor, "is not held nowadays by educated people."

"The second coming of Christ from the skies," says Harry Emerson Fosdick, "is an outmoded phrasing of hope."

"The first Christians looked for the immediate return of Christ and with it the end of the 'present age,'" observes Hugh Burnaby; "we must conclude that the expectation was based on a misapprehension."

"Paul was completely wrong," affirms J. D. Pearse-Higgins, "in his idea of a Second Coming and the sudden transformation of the still living into etheric or spiritual bodies like those of such as had already died and were expected to return on the clouds of heaven with Christ."

So according to theological liberalism, the hope of the Second Coming from the start has been a mistake, an error into which even our Lord himself lapsed and which He passed on to His followers.

It Is a Mystery

The second reply to the hope of Christ's personal return is that it is an inscrutable mystery.

To try to read a book through its covers is hard enough, these doubters say, but it is simplicity itself compared with trying to read the future. They claim that attempting to peer "between the pages of the unopened years" is both impious and impossible.

Though some have tried to do this, these people claim their forecasts have been so vague as to be quite valueless.

Even the Book of Revelation, they tell us, is to be dismissed as "history in hysterics," a document that no one can make heads nor tails of.

Faith in the Second Coming is an effort to find meaning in a mystery, they claim, an effort foredoomed to failure and frustration.

It Is a Myth

The third reply is that the hope of the Second Coming is just a myth.

"It is evident," writes Oliver Chase Quick, "that the notions of a Last Day and a Second Advent are not to be taken literally at all."

"In the New Testament," according to William Barclay, we have "a picture in terms of a world view which is simply no longer tenable. It is seen in terms of a universe where heaven is somewhere above the sky, and from which the Lord comes down, and to which He and His people will go up. We can no longer take this picture literally in the spatial sense of the term. The truth which this picture contains must be symbolic."

"I suppose few of us believe literally in the Second Coming anymore," confesses Hugh Montefiore.

"We pay lip service to the idea in the creeds, but at best we would say it is symbolism."

Thus many maintain that the Advent faith is a mere myth.

It Is a Mighty Manifestation

The fourth and final reply is that our Lord's personal return will be a mighty manifestation.

This faith is firmly grounded on the Word of the God who could not be false without denying His own nature. "It was impossible for God to lie" (Hebrews 6:18).

The Advent faith is no mistake. Nor is it an impenetrable mystery. It is founded on the testimony of One to whose all-knowing mind the future is already a present reality, and to whom therefore its events are no mystery. "I am God, and there is none like me; declaring the end from the beginning, and from ancient times the things that are not yet done" (Isaiah 46:9, 10).

The prospect of Christ's reappearance on this planet is so rooted in passage after passage of the Bible, and these passages are so obviously factual, that to interpret them other than literally would be almost to treat them as if they were untrue.

The New Testament speaks of the "promise of his coming" (2 Peter 3:4). Some promises may be made to be broken; but not this one. Jesus really is coming back to earth again!

CHAPTER 3

How Will Jesus Come Back?

WHEN JESUS RETURNS, how will He come? Or has He already come?

Various popular misconceptions and evasions try to explain the precise manner of His advent. It is important to examine these so we know just what we are talking about when we speak of the Second Coming.

Second Coming Not His Earthly Ministry

The first misconception of the Second Coming is that of those who say they find it fulfilled in the *earthly ministry of our Lord*.

The most distinguished representative of this school of thought is C. H. Dodd with his idea of "realized eschatology."

In his *The Parables of the Kingdom* he writes:

"It seems possible to give to all the eschatological parables of Jesus an application within the context of His ministry. They were intended to enforce His appeal to men to recognize that the kingdom of God was present in all its momentous consequences, and that by their conduct in the presence of this tremendous crisis they would judge themselves as faithful or unfaithful, wise or foolish.

"When the crisis was past, they [the parables] were adapted by the church to enforce its appeal to men to

18

prepare for the second and final world crisis which it believed to be approaching.''

Dodd thus related the teaching of Jesus about the last things to Christ's historic mission, referring them to our Lord's first coming and not to His second coming.

Second Coming Not Pentecost

The second misconception confuses our Saviour's personal return with *Pentecost*.

Now there can be no doubt that Pentecost was the coming of God in a new way into the world; it was not, however, the emergence of the Second Person of the Trinity.

Pentecost was not the *Parousia*. Yet some do confuse them.

''What the Ephesian teacher (the author of the fourth Gospel) is trying to say to his Greek Christian readers,'' suggests George Hedley in *The Symbols of the Faith*, ''is that the effective presence of the Holy Ghost is all the second coming of Christ that we need or ought to want.''

Is that really so? How then does this very same New Testament writer report our Lord himself as saying: ''I will pray the Father, and he will give you *another* Comforter''? (John 14:16).

And is not William Hoste's inquiry precisely to the point: ''How could the coming of the Spirit, which depended on Christ's departure, be the same as Christ's return? 'If I depart, I will send him unto you' (John 16:7).''

A fatal blow is delivered to this false identification of Pentecost with the Rapture by the fact that long after the descent of the Spirit had taken place, we still find New Testament authors pointing *forward* to the Second Coming.

19

Second Coming Not Fall of Jerusalem

The third misconception equates the Second Coming with the *fall of Jerusalem* in A.D. 70.

That was indeed one of the blackest pages of Israel's history. For 4 years the holy city was besieged by the hordes of Titus, the Roman general. After its capitulation, he laid it waste. Could this be the Second Coming?

"One author taking that view," writes Thomas Waugh, "actually says that the Rapture occurred on that occasion, and that amid the cataclysmic struggles of the time the fact was not noted!"

Do the Advent prophecies of Christ refer to the destruction of Jerusalem at this period? It is difficult to resist this conclusion in the light of the following words of the Lord himself: "This generation shall not pass, till all these things be fulfilled" (Matthew 24:34).

Moreover, no Christian perished in the overthrow of the Jewish capital. Heeding our Lord's warning, and sensing their imminent peril, they fled to Pella, on the other side of the Jordan River, and escaped.

Nevertheless there is in the interpretation of Biblical prophecy what may be called a principle of "double fulfillment" or even "multiple fulfillment." The fact that a part of a certain prophecy has come to pass at one point of history does not preclude the possibility that its complete fulfillment awaits future realization.

Second Coming Not an "Inner Return"

The fourth misconception is that which thinks of the Second Coming in terms of *Christ's indwelling of the believer.*

According to neorationalist theologians, Jesus will not come back to earth personally and literally. He returns only in the lives of those who enshrine His principles. Adolf Deissmann actually speaks of Christ's "inner return."

Well, what they say is true—to a degree. There is such a thing as the interior coming of Christ.

Alexander Maclaren speaks of it thus: "When I open my eyes, the light comes in; when I dilate my lungs, the air comes in; when I open my heart, Christ comes in."

But this coming of Christ to the human heart is not at all the same as His coming in the heavens.

Second Coming Not Spiritual Presence

The fifth misconception of the personal return of the Redeemer is that which claims to find its fulfillment in *Christ's spiritual presence in the Church.*

"Where two or three are gathered together in my name, there am I in the midst of them," Jesus said (Matthew 18:20). That mystic presence is a fact; no child of God questions its reality.

Yet I often wonder how people who have no difficulty in accepting as true the universal and eternal presence of Jesus in His church can consistently refuse to believe in His personal presence at one particular point in space and time!

To me it seems much easier to believe such a visible, local reappearance of our Lord than His simultaneous manifestation of himself to His people in all parts of the world!

If anything is clear in the New Testament, it is that Christ's physical body is not now on earth at all.

The numerous references to the Ascension make this unmistakably plain. Never since then has our Lord appeared in the world in bodily form. Whenever subsequently seen, He was always viewed in another dimension of being.

Stephen saw Him standing at the right hand of God (Acts 7:55).

Saul saw Him in a blaze of light in the Syrian sky (Acts 9:3).

John saw Him in the midst of the throne of heaven (Revelation 5:6).

Peter spoke to the magistrates in Jerusalem of "Jesus Christ . . . whom the heaven must receive until the times of restitution of all things" (Acts 3:20,21).

Our Lord has not come back physically since the day of His departure from Mount Olivet, and He will not come back to earth until His feet again alight on that same hallowed spot.

His spiritual presence in His church is definitely not the Second Coming.

Second Coming Not Death

The sixth misconception of the Advent prophecies construes them as being connected with the *death of the Christian*.

It is, of course, an immensely comforting fact that Christ does come for the believer in the hour of his passing. Christian biography is full of examples.

But one passage in the New Testament places beyond all reasonable dispute the point that the death of the Christian is not the coming of Christ. That passage is John 21:20-23: "Then Peter, turning about, seeth the disciple whom Jesus loved following . . . and said, Lord, and what shall this man do? Jesus saith unto him, If I will that he tarry till I come, what is that to thee? follow thou me. Then went this saying abroad among the brethren that that disciple should not die."

In this passage the death of the Christian and the second coming of Christ are set in logical opposition: "If I will that he tarry *till I come*. . . . Then went this saying abroad . . . that that disciple should not die."

E. Buckhurst Pinch sums this up succinctly: "There is no Scripture in the whole of the New Testament which declares that Christ comes for us when we die. We go to be with Him, which is far better."

A Literal Return

By a process of elimination, then, we have arrived at the conclusion that the only valid constructions which can be placed upon the Biblical references to our Lord's return are those which *interpret it with the strictest literalness*.

The New Testament is insistent about this. To cite only three texts:

"This same Jesus, which is taken up from you into heaven, shall so come in like manner as ye have seen him go into heaven" (Acts 1:11).

"For this we say unto you by the word of the Lord, that we which are alive and remain unto the coming of the Lord shall not prevent [precede] them which are asleep. For the Lord himself shall descend from heaven with a shout, with the voice of the archangel, and with the trump of God" (1 Thessalonians 4:15, 16).

"Behold, he cometh with clouds; and every eye shall see him" (Revelation 1:7).

What can such words signify but a personal, physical, local, visible reentry into human history by the Man in God's plan?

At the funeral of Sir Winston Churchill I watched David Ben-Gurion, former premier of Israel, walking in slow procession beside Charles DeGaulle.

Looking at Ben-Gurion I said to myself, "Some day, and that not far distant, I expect to see the face of Jesus Christ, Israel's heaven-appointed King, more closely and clearly than I now do the features of her one-time prime minister."

Jesus is coming back as literally as that!

23

CHAPTER 4

Why I Believe Jesus Is Coming

JESUS CHRIST is coming back to this earth.

The Bible is the infallible Word of God and it proclaims in no uncertain terms the approaching reappearance in history of our blessed Lord. One in every 30 verses in the Scripture predicts our Lord's return. For every mention of His first advent there are eight allusions to His second advent.

Of course, some people who call themselves Christian do not subscribe to the view that such passages are to be taken literally. They regard them as pictorial, figurative, symbolic. They spiritualize them, allegorize them, demythologize them—until they emasculate them of all real meaning.

Let me list five reasons why I personally believe that the New Testament prophecies of the Second Coming are to be accepted with utmost literalness.

Jesus Said He Would Return

First, I believe that Jesus Christ is coming back to earth because He himself said so.

Take the following plain statements:

"I will come again" (John 14:3).

"I will see you again" (John 16:22).

"Behold, I come quickly" (Revelation 22:7).

As James Culcross expressed it, "If Christ were not to come, He would break His Word. No fewer than 21 times in the New Testament He specifically referred to His second coming."

My best Friend has told me He is coming back, and I believe what He says.

I do not look for a disembodied wraith, nor an ectoplasmic emanation, nor a thin apparition. I await the real Jesus who ascended from Olivet and is to return before long to that very spot.

"Jesus Christ [is] the same yesterday, today, and for ever" (Hebrews 13:8). And it is *"this same* Jesus" (Acts 1:11) whose advent I rapturously anticipate.

The Resurrection

Second, I believe the Lord Jesus will come back because He has already returned to the world.

It is not the habit of the dead, however noble or illustrious, to revisit the earth. Nobody expects Winston Churchill or John F. Kennedy to reappear in human history. They are dead and gone.

But there is one historic Character, incomparably greater than all the others, who has come back. He arose from the dead. His name is Jesus Christ. His resurrection is a prelude to and a pledge of the Rapture.

People Are Praying for His Return

Third, I believe the Lord Jesus will come back because more people now than ever are praying passionately for His return.

Some who are praying for His return seem to be the most unlikely people.

In a hotel in southern Spain I saw a crowd of young people bunched around a jukebox. It was blaring a tune whose words seemed to entrance them. The title of the song was "Jesus, Come Back to Your World."

The only sort of evangelism making any global impact today has the Second Coming as a salient component of its message. Multitudes are being converted through hearing this message. And on each of them rests the responsibility of praying continually for our Lord's return.

"Even so, come, Lord Jesus" is the last prayer in the Bible (Revelation 22:20). But it should be the first prayer on the lips of every believer.

There is good ground for contending that today more people are offering that prayer than at any other time in history.

Signs of the Times

Fourth, I believe the Lord Jesus will come back because all the Biblical prophetic fingers point that way.

Discerning observers cannot fail to see around them the signs of the times because we are living in the time of the signs.

To the disciples who asked, "What shall be the sign of thy coming, and of the end of the world?" (Matthew 24:3), Jesus revealed that in the last days there would be signs in the sun. Billy Graham quoted the Skylab astronauts as reporting that, looking through their telescopes, they saw "an explosion on the sun equal to a hundred million atomic blasts. It created a mushroom cloud larger than five earths."

Jesus further foretold there would be signs on the moon. That also is happening. The appearance of man on that lonely sphere is the most impressive of all. And the Russian threat to stain the moon's surface red vividly reminds us of the scriptural prediction that the moon shall be turned into blood (Acts 2:20).

Jesus also asserted there would be wars and rumors of wars. How true that is. And world powers are increasing the amounts they spend on armaments.

Jesus said there would be signs in Israel. In our day we have seen the homing instinct of the Jewish people functioning in a fashion to which there is no historic parallel.

And so one might go on and on. Nowadays we are looking not *for* signs of Christ's second coming, but *at* them. They abound on every hand. And our blessed Lord directed: "When these things begin to come to pass, then look up, and lift up your heads; for your redemption draweth nigh" (Luke 21:28).

Is the World Doomed?

Finally, I believe that the Lord Jesus is coming back to this world because, if He doesn't, there will be no world to come back to.

It is not fanatical alarmists who say so, but sober men, leading philosophers and scientists.

Bertrand Russell feared that the end would come through nuclear explosion. "I wouldn't give a 50-50 chance that one person will be alive on this planet 40 years from now," he declared.

The Bible pictures just such a catastrophe: "Men were scorched with great heat, and blasphemed the name of God" (Revelation 16:9).

It may end as ecologist Barry Commoner forecasts— by chemical pollution.

"We synthesized and disseminated new insecticides," he said, "before anyone learned they also kill birds and might be harmful to people. We introduced synthetic detergents and put billions of pounds into the

27

surface waters before we realized that they would not be degraded in our disposal systems and would thus pollute our water supplies. We run the risk of destroying this planet as a suitable place for human habitation.''

The Bible touches on that too. It says, ''The earth has been polluted by the dwellers on its face'' (Isaiah 24:5, Moffatt).

It may end, as Julian Huxley warned, through food shortages, occasioned by overpopulation.

''If the current birthquake continues,'' he continued, ''humanity cannot survive more than another 35 years.''

It has been responsibly estimated that by the turn of the century earth's population will have almost doubled itself and will exceed the staggering total of 7 billion! According to economists, this is too many mouths to feed, and masses will starve to death.

To this likewise the Word of God points: ''There shall be famines . . . in divers places'' (Matthew 24:7). Already they have begun. Every time the clock ticks, somebody somewhere dies of starvation.

But the world is not going to end in any of these woeful ways. The Lord Jesus is coming, and all those gloomy forecasts do is to highlight the imminence of His return.

If He does not come soon, He will be too late. If He does not return to the world before long, there will be no world to return to.

So I believe that Christ may reenter history at any moment, and those who are His will be caught up to be with Him forever.

CHAPTER 5

When Jesus Comes for His Own

FOR HIS OWN Jesus has completely transformed the nature of death.

How beautifully and reassuringly He referred to it: "Carried by the angels" (Luke 16:22); "today . . . in paradise" (Luke 23:43); falling asleep (John 11:11).

About this last figure Hogg and Vine comment in their *Expository Notes:* "As the sleeper does not cease to exist while his body sleeps, so the dead person continues to exist despite his absence from the region in which those who remain can communicate with him. And as sleep is known to be temporary, so the death of the body will be found to be so. Sleep has its waking; death will have its resurrection."

God will finally demolish man's last enemy by delivering His people from its power. "For the trumpet shall sound, and the dead shall be raised incorruptible" (1 Corinthians 15:52). They will be no longer disembodied, but "clothed upon with [their] house [habitation] which is from heaven" (2 Corinthians 5:2).

S. Baring-Gould expressed it:

On the Resurrection morning
   Soul and body meet again;
No more sorrow, no more weeping,
   No more pain.

29

Here awhile they must be parted,
  And the flesh its Sabbath keep,
Waiting in a holy calmness
  Fast asleep.

For a while the tired body
  Lies as still as if unborn,
Till there breaks the last, the brightest
  Easter morn.

"The dead in Christ shall rise" (1 Thessalonians 4:16). How starkly Paul stated the stupendous fact.

He explained further in Philippians 3:20, 21: "We look for the Saviour, the Lord Jesus Christ; who shall change our vile body [*the body that belongs to our low estate*, Moffatt], that it may be fashioned like unto his glorious body"—the body that came from the womb of Mary and from the tomb of Joseph of Arimathea.

In his *The Substance of the Christian Faith*, R. G. Macintyre makes a significant remark about this. He says: "Paul did not argue for a bodily resurrection but for a resurrection body, a very different thing."

We may concede that is true, but the concession must be made with caution. According to the New Testament, there *is* a connection between the body laid in the dust and the body raised in the new splendor of immortality. Our Lord himself established that link: "The hour is coming, in the which all that are *in the graves* shall hear his voice [of the Son of man], and shall come forth" (John 5:28, 29).

The parodox is that the bodies resurrected will be the same as those deposited in the sepulcher—yet different.

That is not so hard to understand as it might at first appear. God gave you a body when you were born. It weighed only a few pounds and was very different in size and shape from the one you have now. But when you look at a photograph of yourself as an infant in your mother's arms, you have no doubt that that tiny body is yours. "That's me," you say.

So on the Resurrection morning. The risen form will be identifiably continuous with the corpse laid in the clay, yet now released forever from all disease, deformity, disfiguration, and death.

What a glad reunion will occur! There will be instant, rapturous, mutual recognition.

A fine Christian lady came to me in deep distress. Her mother, then over 90, had become senile and no longer recognized her. To be treated as a stranger by the one with whom she had the tenderest of all earthly ties was a trial the daughter could hardly endure.

"Do you think Mother will know me in heaven?" she asked.

I referred her to the scene at the transfiguration of Christ (Matthew 17:1-8). Obviously, Peter had never seen Moses and Elijah until they appeared before him there. The former had been buried and the latter translated hundreds of years prior to Peter's birth. Yet Jesus evidently did not need to introduce them. He didn't say: "Peter, this is Moses; this is Elijah." Introductions were superfluous. Instantly Peter realized who they were.

Just so, I sought to assure my friend, will it be on the Resurrection morning with her and her beloved mother. Recognition will be instinctive and immediate. For in the words of the German aphorism: "Those who live in the Lord never see each other for the last time."

"Death is swallowed up in victory" (1 Corinthians 15:54). As Andrew Bonar said: "Death swallows us up now, but we shall see Death swallowed up at the grave's mouth on the Resurrection morning."

We Shall Be Changed

The Transformation of the living Christians will be no less literal. ''We shall all be changed'' (1 Corinthians 15:51). ''The Lord Jesus Christ . . . shall change our vile bodies'' (Philippians 3:20, 21). One generation of Christians will cheat the undertaker!

''We which are alive and remain'' is how Paul described it. Not having died, they will not need to be resurrected, but they will need to be changed. Their bodies will have to be adapted to a new dimension of being, just as the tiny grub in the stagnant pool needs to be radically changed to become the filmy, flowerlike creature with gossamer wings that flies in the summer sun.

Change is, of course, the order of life. Time is transforming us, and grace is transfiguring the Christian. ''We all, with open face beholding as in a glass the glory of the Lord, are changed into the same image from glory to glory, even as by the Spirit of the Lord'' (2 Corinthians 3:18).

But on the day of the Resurrection that gradual transformation will be replaced by a sudden, dramatic change—''in a moment, in the twinkling of an eye'' (1 Corinthians 15:52).

A simple illustration may help here. Suppose that Annigoni, the celebrated Italian artist, is commissioned to paint another portrait of Queen Elizabeth II. Session after session will be arranged, and touch by touch the paint will be transferred by the master's hand to the canvas, until at long last the royal likeness will emerge.

But now suppose that Annigoni has with him, when his work is completed, a camera and he takes a colored snapshot of the queen. In a flash her image is transmitted to the sensitized film. What had taken many months, perhaps years, to paint is reproduced in the twinkling of an eye!

Our change will be instantaneous. "When he shall appear, we shall be like him; for we shall see him as he is" (1 John 3:2).

A man once asked a Christian for a photograph of himself. The Christian replied: "I'm sorry that you asked for it now."

"Why?" the man responded.

"Because later I expect to be more like Jesus Christ!"

Instantly the living saints will be changed. The sight of the Saviour will transform them in a split second into His image.

The Summons

Then will sound the summons to arise. The resurrected Christian dead and the transformed Christian living will be translated together. Not even the apostles will take precedence in that ascent by a fraction of a second over the simplest believer. *Together!* That is the operative word. All at once.

An old saint, at the point of death, was urged by her son: "Hang on a bit, Mother. Jesus is coming soon, and we can all go up together."

"Oh, no," she said. "I think I'll just go now and avoid the rush!"

But though the countless multitudes will ascend at once, there will be no congestion, no collision in the skies—any more than there is with the rays that stream from the sun.

And thus our Lord's sublime words will be invested with new and marvelous meaning: "He that believeth in me, though he were dead, yet shall he live [that is the raising of the dead saints at the Rapture], and

33

whosoever liveth and believeth in me shall never die [that is the transformation of the living saints]" (John 11:25, 26).

Yes, the Rapture will be literal, not figurative. It will all form part of the solid stuff of history, occurring at an actual date marked on the calendar and at a moment shown on the clock.

That same Jesus who, ascending,
Passed through heaven's portals wide,
Soon shall come from heaven descending
To receive His Blood-bought bride.

Yes, himself and not another,
We shall see His form most fair;
And His own, caught up together,
Glad shall meet Him in the air.

CHAPTER 6
Believers at the Bema

AFTER BELIEVERS have been raptured to be with the Lord forever, they will appear before the Lord at the Bema.

What is the Bema?

The term is Greek and in some English Bibles is translated "judgment seat."*

That rendering appears to me to be too judicial. The original expression was borrowed not from the realm of law but from the Olympic games. It signified the dais on which the judges sat and from which they commanded an unobstructed view of the course and competitors. They could thus justly award the laurel wreath to the winner or disqualify other entrants who had violated the rules or failed to win a place.

Contestants had to appear before the chair of the president of the games so their performance could be officially assessed and announced.

---

*Four great judgments are ahead in prophecy. The first, the subject of this chapter, is the Bema, also called the Judgment Seat of Christ (2 Corinthians 5:10). The second will be the Judgment of the Living Nations (Matthew 25:21, 22). The third will be that of regathered Israel (Ezekiel 20:33, ff.). The fourth will be the judgment of the unbelievers at the Great White Throne (Revelation 20:11, 12).

So it is important to remember that the term used for the evaluation of believers after the Rapture is not *thronos* but *bema*.

Contrasting the judgment of the unbelievers at the Great White Throne and the judgment of believers at the Bema, A. J. Pollock likened the former to a murder trial and the latter to a flower show. At both judgment is dispensed. But the object of one is to establish guilt, while the other is to ascertain merit. The best the one can do is to *acquit;* the best the other can do is *acclaim.* There are no prizes at a murder trial; there are at a flower show.

The Bema is a judgment for Christians only. It is not a judgment of sin but of service. Our sins have already been judged.

From first to last the Christian life is a period of probation. We have been given specific work to do, lessons to learn, problems to solve, achievements to attain, and objectives to gain. At the Bema our lives will be subjected to the final divine appraisal.

The Word of God assures us of this again and again:

"Thou shalt be recompensed at the resurrection of the just" (Luke 14:14).

"The Father . . . hath committed all judgment unto the Son" (John 5:22).

"Every one of us shall give account of himself to God" (Romans 14:12).

"For we must all appear before the judgment seat of Christ; that every one may receive the things done in his body, according to that he hath done, whether it be good or bad" (2 Corinthians 5:10).

Other passages carry across this same theme, for throughout the New Testament the truth of this final audit is firmly and frequently taught.

The theme is both thrilling and threatening—thrilling because of the awards that will be given there; threatening because of the irreparable loss which may be sustained. No Christian will be lost at the Bema—but he may suffer loss.

Think first of the positive side. There are to be rewards.

The New Testament does not despise nor discourage the concept of rewards. It often enjoins moral duty and encourages noble effort by enlisting the aid of moral incentives. It points to the sure and just apportionment of such rewards.

The Bible teaches that these rewards will be: (1) personally conferred; (2) proportionally allotted; and (3) permanently awarded.

Personally Conferred

First, they will be *personally conferred*.

When the New Testament writers exultantly refer to the rewards they expect to receive at the Bema, not a little of their excitement stems from the fact that it will be from the Lord himself that they will receive these gifts. "The Lord, the righteous judge, shall give me [the crown] at that day" (2 Timothy 4:8).

Proportionally Allotted

The rewards will be *proportionally allotted*. There will be "gold, silver, precious stones" (1 Corinthians 3:12). There is such a thing as "a full reward" (2 John 8).

As Christians we are saved by grace—and by grace alone. But let us never forget that we shall be finally judged by works.

Leith Samuel, in *Remember, I Am Coming Soon,* writes: "The fact that when we are 'in Christ' there is

37

no condemnation for our sins does not mean there is no examination of our works.''

It will not be all commendation at the Bema; there will be condemnation too.

''Every man's work shall be made manifest: for the day shall declare it, because it shall be revealed by fire; and the fire shall try every man's work of what sort it is'' (1 Corinthians 3:13).

''If any man's work abide which he hath built thereon, he shall receive a reward. If any man's work shall be burned, he shall suffer loss: but he himself shall be saved; yet so as by fire'' (1 Corinthians 3:14, 15).

So there is the tragic possibility of disqualification. Even the apostle Paul feared it: ''I keep under my body, and bring it into subjection: lest that by any means, when I have preached to others, I myself should be a castaway'' (1 Corinthians 9:27).

The worst penalty which can be inflicted on a runner is that he should not be first to breast the tape. Thus we find the writer to the Hebrews giving some excellent advice: ''Wherefore, seeing we also are compassed about with so great a cloud of witnesses, let us lay aside every weight, and the sin which doth so easily beset us; and let us run with patience the race that is set before us, looking unto Jesus the author and finisher of our faith'' (Hebrews 12:1, 2).

Permanently Awarded

The rewards distributed at the Bema will be *permanently awarded*. The decisions of the divine court are never reversed or annulled.

It is a solemn thought. No soul will be consigned to hell from the Bema. The judgment will not be of sins but of service. But what responsible Christian can contemplate, without profound soul-searching, the possibility, that the works of a lifetime will go up in flames—the result being eternal impoverishment for the one who performed them?

We can build with gold, silver, and precious stones; or we can build with wood, hay, and stubble. Thomas Guthrie says that you can keep pure gold in a furnace for a thousand years and it will not lose a fraction of its substance in the flame. But how long does it take straw to flare up and fade away forever?

Roger Bannister, the famous British athlete, was the first man to run a mile in 4 minutes. Three months later John Landy topped his record by 1.4 seconds.

Later the two were competing in a great race. As they entered the last lap, they had far outdistanced all other competitors. Landy was ahead. It appeared he would win.

But as he approached the tape, curiosity got the better of him. "Where is Bannister?" he kept asking himself. For a split second he turned to find out. And in that second Bannister flashed past him and won the race.

Reviewing the race later, Landy told a *Time* magazine correspondent: "If I hadn't looked back, I'd have won the race."

How unspeakably tragic it will be to fail to gain a full reward.

In the light of the warnings of the Word, let us seek to walk daily "in the print of Christ's shoe," scrutinizing our motives, buying up every opportunity, and doing all in our power to promote the interests of Christ's cause and kingdom.

CHAPTER 7

Faultless Before the Throne

JUST AS a man, who has wooed and won the heart of a beautiful woman in a distant land, brings her home to his father's house and proudly introduces her, so will the Lord Jesus present His perfect Church, "not having spot, or wrinkle, or any such thing" (Ephesians 5:27) to His Heavenly Father.

The Presentation of the Church

Several passages of Scripture mention this presentation of the Church. Here are the principal references:

"He which raised up the Lord Jesus shall raise up us also by Jesus, and shall present us with you" (2 Corinthians 4:14).

"That he might present it [the Church] to himself a glorious church, not having spot, or wrinkle, or any such thing; but that it should be holy and without blemish" (Ephesians 5:27).

"You . . . hath he reconciled . . . to present you holy and unblamable and unreprovable in his sight" (Colossians 1:21, 22).

"Now unto him that is able to keep you from falling, and to present you faultless before the presence of his glory, with exceeding joy, to the only wise God, our Saviour, be glory and majesty, dominion and power, both now and ever. Amen" (Jude 24, 25).

A striking and impressive illustration of this is provided by a spectacular scene in the life of Bertel Thorvaldsen, the distinguished Danish sculptor.

Although born in Denmark, Thorvaldsen spent most of his adult life abroad. And always he was working away with plaster of paris or marble, molding or carving those massive and magnificent masterpieces which have won for him a place in the van of sculptural achievement.

As old age came on, however, his heart turned homeward. He decided to go back to Denmark. But he did not return empty-handed. With him he brought as many as he could acquire of his own superb sculptures and plaster casts.

Hiring a fleet of vessels, he took into Copenhagen harbor the treasure of his genius.

As the ships entered the haven, flags flew, bunting streamed, bells rang, and trumpets blew. Out from the wharf to meet them came a flotilla of gaily decorated barges, in one of which sailed the Danish king and members of the royal family; on the other boats were members of the senate, burgesses of the city, and high-ranking officials of all kinds.

Then, amid tumultuous excitement, Thorvaldsen presented his masterpieces to the king, who graciously received them in the name of the nation.

Afterwards the sculptures were placed on open wagons and paraded through the crowded streets. The air rang with the rapturous shouts of the people. Finally the statues were placed in a one-man museum where they are still on public display.

What a graphic portrayal of Christ presenting His perfected Church to the Father, "That in the ages to come he might show the exceeding riches of his grace, in his kindness toward us, through Christ Jesus"

(Ephesians 2:7). Our hearts thrill to the thought of Jesus fashioning by His grace the lives of men and women in all parts of the world and finally displaying them without fault or flaw to "the King, eternal, immortal, invisible" (1 Timothy 1:17) amid the exulting hosts of heaven.

The Marriage Supper

According to Ephesians 5:27, 31, 32, the presentation of the Church to the Father will immediately precede the Marriage Supper of the Lamb.

Revelation 19:7-9 says: "Let us be glad and rejoice, and give honor to him: for the marriage of the Lamb is come, and his wife hath made herself ready. And to her was granted that she should be arrayed in fine linen, clean and white: for the fine linen is the righteousness of saints. And he saith unto me, Write, blessed are they which are called unto the marriage supper of the Lamb."

First, let us identify the *Bridegroom*. We have no difficulty here. He is the Lord Jesus Christ himself. Repeatedly in the Bible He is represented in that role. "Then came to him the disciples of John, saying, Why do we and the Pharisees fast oft, but Thy disciples fast not? And Jesus said unto them, Can the children of the bridechamber mourn, as long as the bridegroom is with them? but the days will come, when the bridegroom shall be taken from them, and then shall they fast" (Matthew 9:14, 15).

It is highly significant that, alone among the leaders of the great world religions, Jesus never married. Confucius, founder of the faith of China, was wed at 19. Buddha was a married man. Muhammad was no bachelor.

But Jesus never entered the matrimonial state. Why? He knew that His wedding date had been fixed in the mind of God "before the hills in order stood or earth received her frame." He knew that He was to be married to that "chaste virgin," the Church, His spiritual spouse. Jesus is to be the eternal Bridegroom.

Who is the *bride* of Christ? She is the Church, and no one else. Positive proof of this is provided on page after page of the New Testament:

"I have espoused you to one husband, that I may present you as a chaste virgin to Christ" (2 Corinthians 11:2).

"For this cause shall a man leave his father and mother, and shall be joined unto his wife, and they two shall be one flesh. This is a great mystery: but I speak concerning Christ and the church" (Ephesians 5:31, 32).

Yes! there can be no doubt that the bride is the Church.

Is it possible to ascertain what she is wearing at the wedding?

"Unto her was granted," we read, "to be arrayed in fine linen, clean and white" (Revelation 19:8). Then an explanatory note is added: "For the fine linen is the righteousness of saints."

The term *righteousness* in that context might be better rendered "righteous acts." The suggestion is that the bride is to have a hand in weaving her own wedding gown, for, as John Taylor Smith liked to say: "We *weave* on earth what we *wear* in heaven."

Unmarried females used to be called "spinsters." At one time the expression was much more appropriate than it is now. Then ladies were in the habit of spinning materials for their trousseaux, so as to have something in their "hope chest."

43

Today the Church is a "spinster." She is preparing now the fabric of that gorgeous robe which she will wear at her heavenly nuptials.

It is true, of course, that she will be concerned about her clothing. What bride isn't? But she will not be preoccupied with her apparel to the exclusion of her beloved Lord.

We have spoken of the Bridegroom and the bride. But what of the guests? Who are they?

About that there are different opinions. Some say they consist of "the godly of all ages prior to Pentecost"; others that they will consist of Tribulation saints; others that they will be converted Jews.

The placing of the bridal supper in the chronology of Biblical prophecy would seem to militate against the possibility of the last two suggestions, and many would want to include the godly of ages preceding Pentecost within the pale of the Church itself, making them thus part of the Bride rather than numbering them among the guests.

Amid the variety of views, however, one thing is certain. Everyone so summoned will be beatified. "Blessed are they which are called unto the marriage supper of the Lamb" (Revelation 19:9).

In His great high-priestly prayer recorded in John 17, our Lord offered the most amazing intercessions on behalf of His Church. He asked: "That they all may be one; as thou, Father, art in me, and I in thee, that they also may be one in us . . . one even as we are one" (John 17: 21, 22).

Paul, as we have noted, compared the communion between Christ and His Church to that of husband and wife, who in marriage become "one flesh" (Ephesians 5:31).

Could language go farther in an effort to convey the ineffableness of the union?

Yet it is vitally important to remember that, intimate beyond imagining as will be the fellowship between the Lord and His own, there is an infinite categorical difference between Creator and creature which will never be transcended. The Church will never become God.

Yet with that sole reservation, we may justly claim that the union and communion will be the closest in the cosmos, save that between the three Persons in the blessed Trinity themselves.

No wonder Samuel Rutherford exclaimed: "Oh, that He would cry to His heavenly trumpeters: 'Make ready! Let us go down and fold together the four corners of the world, and marry the Bride!' " That festal hour may be nearer than we dream.

"Even so, come, Lord Jesus" (Revelation 22:20).

CHAPTER 8

The Unveiling of the Man of Sin

THE WORLD TODAY waits to welcome the best of men and the worst of men.

Christ is coming! Antichrist is coming! And it is immensely significant that in the original text the New Testament uses the same term for both advents. It speaks of the *parousia* of Christ and the *parousia* of Antichrist.

Here is its reference to the former: "The coming of the Lord draweth nigh" (James 5:8). And here is its allusion to the latter: "Then shall that Wicked be revealed . . . whose coming is after the working of Satan with all power and signs and lying wonders" (2 Thessalonians 2:8, 9).

"The devil," says Martin Luther, "is God's ape." Satan is the master-copyist of the cosmos. His age-long policy is to counterfeit and caricature the divine.

It is an astounding exercise to examine the points of parallel between Christ and Antichrist.

Christ is "the Son of Man" (John 12:34). Antichrist is "the son of perdition" (2 Thessalonians 2:3). Christ is "the Good Shepherd" (John 10:14). Antichrist is "the idol shepherd" (Zechariah 11:17).

The duration of Christ's public ministry was 3½ years; the period during which Antichrist will be at his pernicious prime will be 3½ years.

As to the nature of their respective activities, of Christ Acts 2:22 reports that it consisted of "miracles and wonders and signs." Of the activities of Antichrist the New Testament uses the terms, "power and signs and lying wonders" (2 Thessalonians 2:9).

Christ was "wounded for our transgressions" (Isaiah 53:5). Of Antichrist Revelation 13:12 speaks as "the first beast, whose deadly wound was healed."

And before Christ reigns in Jerusalem, Antichrist will reign there, just as Saul, the people's choice, ruled before David, the Lord's choice.

Who, then, is this satanic superman, this counterfeit christ? In the interests of clarity and comprehension, I should like to divide this study into four parts: (1) the portents of Antichrist; (2) the portrait of Antichrist; (3) the partner of Antichrist; and (4) the program of Antichrist.

The Portents of Antichrist

The apostle John reports that even in his day the spirit of Antichrist was already abroad in the world: "Ye have heard that antichrist shall come, even now are there many antichrists" (1 John 2:18). So the dynasty of Antichrist is of long standing. Satan's superman has had many precursors.

Has not each of us, if we are quite honest, an anticipation of Antichrist in his own heart? The Man of Sin is simply the objectification of the sin of man.

The Portrait of Antichrist

The Bible paints it in sharp lines and lurid colors. Let us start with our Lord's own allusion to him. "I am come in my father's name, and ye receive me not: if another shall come in his own name, him ye will receive" (John 5:43).

And here are other scriptural references to the devil's double: "Ten kings . . . shall arise; and another shall rise after them; and he shall be diverse from the first, and he shall subdue three kings. And he shall speak great words against the Most High, and shall wear out the saints of the Most High, and think to change times and laws: and they shall be given into his hand until a time and times and the dividing of time" (Daniel 7:24, 25).*

The name by which he is most frequently mentioned in the Book of Revelation is "the beast." In the original the term is *therion*, and not a few modern translations render this "animal." Personally, I find that rather ludicrous. Would not the best English equivalent of the Greek be "the brute"? Such is the Biblical portrait of Antichrist.

His personality has three dominant characteristics.

He is *attractive*. "All the world wondered after the beast" (Revelation 13:3). He appears to possess a certain mesmeric charm.

Again, He is *articulate*. "There was given unto him a mouth speaking great things" (Revelation 13:5).

And he is *aggressive*. "It was given unto him to make war with the saints, and to overcome them" (Revelation 13:7).

Help toward pinpointing the identity of Antichrist is prophetically provided in Revelation 13:18: "Here is wisdom. Let him that hath understanding count the number of the beast: for it is the number of a man; and his number is six hundred threescore and six."

What is the number of the Beast? In the Book of Revelation, as we have seen, it is 666—a trinity of sixes; that is, according to Biblical numerology, the perfection of humanism.

*See also Daniel 7:8; 8:23-25; 9:26, 27; 11:36-38; 2 Thessalonians 2:3, 4, 8, 9; Revelation 13:1-8, 18.

Whom does the number 666 designate? Human ingenuity has taxed itself to the utmost to interpret this arithmetical puzzle. 666 has been made to stand for Nero, Hitler, and many others.

Difficult as it is now to identify the Man of Sin, it will be easy to do so when the time comes for his showing to the world. The clue will then be furnished for the deciphering of the mysterious number.

The Partner of Antichrist

This is the sinister satellite variously described in Scripture as "the second beast" and "the false prophet." Here is how the Word of God introduces him: "I beheld another beast coming up out of the earth; and he had two horns like a lamb, and he spake as a dragon. And he exerciseth all the power of the first beast before him, and causeth the earth and them that dwell therein to worship the first beast" (Revelation 13:11, 12).

The False Prophet will be the leader of the apostate world church of the future, a fusion of Romanist and ecumenical sectors in organized Christianity.

In contradistinction to the bride of Christ, the Lamb's wife, the New Testament speaks of that infernal institution as "the harlot." From the nature of her tarnished trade a whore must be attractive. If not attractive she will soon be out of business.

Although closely associated with Rome, the False Prophet and his profane organization must not be precisely identified with it. The coming great world church will be bigger than Romanism.

The Program of Antichrist

At this point we must digress a little to remind ourselves how remarkably the stage of world history is now being set for the enactment of the final drama of the age. The contemporary scene has five blocs corresponding exactly to Biblical prediction: (1) repatriated Israel; (2) Rosh, or Russia, the King of the North; (3) the King of the South, the United Arab Republic; (4) the Kings of the East, that awakening giant China and her satellites; and (5) the revived Roman Empire which many connect with the Common Market.

Where does Antichrist fit into this picture? There is no doubt that he will be a glittering personality. "All the world wondered after the beast" (Revelation 13:3). Like his master, Satan, he will transform himself into an "angel of light" (2 Corinthians 11:14).

He will prove himself especially ingratiating to the Israelis and will enter into a 7-year pact with them. He will also encourage them to rebuild their temple and to recommence the rites of their ancestral religion.

That the world is ready to welcome such a leader was dramatically demonstrated by a startling statement made in Paris in October 1957 by Henri Spaak, as secretary-general of the North Atlantic Treaty Organization: "We do not want another committee: we have too many already. What we want is a man of sufficient stature to hold the allegiance of all people and to lift us out of the economic morass into which we are sinking. Send us such a man and, be he god or devil, we will receive him."

Antichrist will be both god and devil—the devil incarnate setting himself up as God.

Are there any signs in human society today of the appearance of such a person? Of course, he will not be publicly revealed until after the rapture of the Church; but since he will then be fitted for world dominion, it is a fair inference that he will be in the world for probably 30 years before that.

Midway through the 7-year period of his pact with the Jews, Antichrist will break its main provisions, throw off his disguise, and appear in his true colors. "He shall exalt himself, and magnify himself above every god" (Daniel 11:36).

The Jews will by this time, under his patronage, have built in Jerusalem a magnificent temple. Rumors have been rife for some while that they are already engaged in preparing for its construction.

It is quite clear from the prophetic Scriptures that there will be a temple in the Holy City during the closing days of this era. Two texts establish that. The first is our Lord's own declaration: "When ye therefore shall see the abomination of desolation, spoken of by Daniel the prophet, stand in the holy place" (Matthew 24:15). The second is Paul's reference to the Man of Sin in 2 Thessalonians 2:4, "Who as God sitteth in the temple of God."

One way or another, the temple will be built before long, but not, it would seem, until after the public appearance of Antichrist.

After 3½ years as world-ruler, the Man of Sin will reveal himself for what he really is. Aided and abetted by his satellite, the False Prophet, he will have his image set up in the temple, and will cause the sacrifice and oblation to cease. This will initiate the period known in the Bible as the Great Tribulation.

CHAPTER 9

The Great Tribulation

Is THERE TO BE a Great Tribulation in the future? About this there are four main views.

Four Views of the Tribulation

1. The Jews believed that what we call the Great Tribulation occurred in September, A.D. 70, when Titus besieged their holy city and destroyed it.

2. Some hold that the Great Tribulation extends during the indefinite period between the death of Christ and the restitution of all things.

3. Philip Mauro taught that the Great Tribulation was the period between the baptism of Jesus and the coming of the Roman prince Titus to attack Jerusalem.

4. Many maintain that the Great Tribulation is a time of terror, still future, in which the current age will culminate.

Proponents of these four points of view can be classified into three broad categories: the preterist, the historicist, and the futurist. Theories 1 and 3 belong to the preterist, theory 2 to the historicist, and theory 4 to the futurist.

Some assert that the *tribulation* may be taken as descriptive of the essential character of the whole Christian life. They quote such texts as these:

"In the world ye shall have tribulation" (John 16:33).

"We must through much tribulation enter into the kingdom of God" (Acts 14:22).

"We told you . . . that we should suffer tribulation" (1 Thessalonians 3:4).

It is true, of course, that tribulation in this world is the lot of the Lord's people, but there are references in the Bible which are so specific and determinate that such a general interpretation cannot adequately cover them.

Another school of historicists construe the phrase "the Great Tribulation" as applying to the epochs of persecution through which the Church has passed through the centuries.

This is Professor Milligan's position. "Nor are we to understand by the Great Tribulation," he writes, "merely a special tribulation at the close of the world's history. It is rather the trials experienced by the saints of God throughout the whole period of their pilgrimage, at one time greater than another, but always great" (quoted by A. E. Richardson in *He Shall Come Again*).

The futurists see the Great Tribulation as a time yet to come when the earth will go through the darkest days it has ever known.

To this the following passages of Scripture point unmistakably:

"Behold, the Lord cometh out of his place to punish the inhabitants of the earth for their iniquity" (Isaiah 26:21).

"Behold, the Lord maketh the earth empty, and maketh it waste, and turneth it upside down" (Isaiah 24:1).

"There shall be a time of trouble, such as never was since there was a nation even to that same time" (Daniel 12:1).

53

"Alas! for that day is great, so that none is like it: it is even the time of Jacob's trouble" (Jeremiah 30:7).

"Then shall be great tribulation, such as was not since the beginning of the world to this time, no, nor ever shall be" (Matthew 24:21).

"These are they which came out of great tribulation" (Revelation 7:14).

Such verses obviously allude not to tribulation in general, but to an event yet future, unique in its barbarity and horror in the history of the human race.

Yet it is not wholly punitive in its purpose. It aims at separating the wheat from the chaff in human society. The Greek word *thlipsis* of which "tribulation" is the English translation conveyed the thought of pressing grapes in a winepress, but the Latin term *tribulum* is more in line with our thought here, for it means a flail, what my Scottish forefathers would have called "a flinging-tree," an implement made of two pieces of wood tied together at two ends with a leather thong and used in threshing grain.

It will be a bitter harvest. The whole world will go through the mill, but for the Jews it will be a period of peculiar peril and persecution.

Jeremiah designated it "the time of Jacob's trouble." It will be the last awful outbreak of anti-Semitism.

The Length of the Tribulation

We may agree, then, that the Great Tribulation is still to transpire, but on what grounds do we base the assumption it will last for approximately 7 years?

In his book *Scared to Death*, John Barker, a consultant psychologist, uses a striking figure to describe people of extraordinary sensitivity who are able to predict in advance disasters about to happen.

54

He calls them "human seismographs." Of these the Hebrew prophets were conspicuous examples.

This is demonstrably true of Daniel. He felt the tremors of the Great Tribulation though it had not yet taken place.

While at prayer one evening he was told by the angel Gabriel:

"Seventy weeks are decreed upon thy people and upon thy holy city, to finish transgression and to make an end of sins, and to make reconciliation for iniquity, and to bring in everlasting righteousness, and to seal up vision and prophecy, and to anoint the Most Holy. Know therefore and discern that from the going forth of the commandment to restore and to build Jerusalem, unto Messiah the Prince, shall be seven weeks, and threescore and two weeks; it shall be built again with street and moat, even in troublous times. And after threescore and two weeks shall Messiah be cut off, and shall have nothing; and the people of the prince that shall come shall destroy the city and the sanctuary; and his end thereof shall be with a flood, and even unto the end shall be war, desolations are determined. And he [that is, Antichrist, 'the prince that shall come'] shall make a firm covenant with many for one week" (Daniel 9:24-27, marginal readings).

Commenting on this, Sir Robert Anderson asks: "What was the length of the period intervening between the issuing of the decree to rebuild Jerusalem and the public advent of Messiah the prince—between March 14, 445 B.C. and April 6, A.D. 32? The interval contained exactly 173,880 days, or seven times 69 prophetic years of 360 days, the first 69 weeks of Gabriel's prophecy" (*The Coming Prince*).

But what of the 70th week? Futurists believe there is a break in the chronological continuity of that prophetic passage midway through verse 26—that is, between the reference to Messiah's being cut off and the coming of the prince who is Antichrist—and that, as it is connected with the end-time and has not yet transpired, it is bound to be still future.

Not all prophetic scholars agree. E. P. Cachemaille, for instance, in *The Prophetic Outlook Today*, crosses swords with Sir Robert Anderson on this point. "The 70th week, or any part of it," Cachemaille writes, "may not be wrenched away from the other 69 and relegated to some distant future: it cleaves to the 69th. The 70 weeks, being a definite measurement of time, run on continuously from one to 70, the last week being divided into two halves; otherwise the measurement would have no meaning. Suppose you have a rod 70 inches long. From any fixed point you can lay the rod in any direction, and the point its end reaches will always be just 70 inches from the starting point. But suppose you break off from the rod 1 inch, or ½ inch, and then tie between the two broken ends a long piece of elastic. You can stretch the broken piece away to any distance you please, but you have destroyed the measurement of 70 inches."

Despite Cachemaille's clever illustration, there is Biblical warrant for making the break in the prophetic passage where futurists make it.

Our Lord himself did exactly the same thing in the synagogue at Nazareth. When uttering His great manifesto on that occasion, He did not complete the quotation from Isaiah 61:1, 2. He closed the book before He closed the sentence. He put a full stop or at least a dash where the prophet put a comma.

"There was delivered unto him the book of the prophet Isaiah. And when he had opened the book, he found the place where it was written, The Spirit of the

56

Lord is upon me, because he hath anointed me to preach the gospel to the poor; he hath sent me to heal the broken-hearted, to preach deliverance to the captives, and recovering of sight to the blind, to set at liberty them that are bruised, to preach the acceptable year of the Lord. And he closed the book, and he gave it again to the minister, and sat down'' (Luke 4:17-20).

In the Old Testament the prophet immediately goes on, ''and the day of vengeance of our God.'' There is the highest precedent for inserting this parenthesis in the passage, but Jesus didn't include that part of the prophecy when He said: ''This day is this Scripture fulfilled in your ears'' (Luke 4:21).

So the Great Tribulation is roughly a 7-year period yet to come during which Antichrist will be a dazzling dictator controlling the destinies of the world. For the first 3½ years he will be admired and applauded; but, as we have seen, at the expiration of that period he will throw away his mask and show himself as he really is.

The Events of the Tribulation

Aided and abetted by his lieutenant, the False Prophet, he will have the image of himself set up in the temple at Jerusalem, compelling people on pain of death to offer to him divine honors. This is the signal for the outbreak of the Great Tribulation as such.

The two witnesses will appear in Jerusalem, bear their brave witness and be martyred. Their dead bodies will lie exposed to the television cameras, for the gaping world to gaze at, before they are resurrected and translated to heaven. Many maintain that these witnesses are reincarnations of either Enoch and Elijah or Moses and Elijah.

Here is how the Word of God describes that period:

57

"In the midst of the week he shall cause the sacrifice and the oblation to cease, and for the overspreading of abominations he shall make it desolate, even until the consummation, and that determined shall be poured upon the desolate" (Daniel 9:27).

"From the time that the daily sacrifice shall be taken away, and the abomination that maketh desolate set up, there shall be a thousand two hundred and ninety days" (Daniel 12:11).

"When ye therefore shall see the abomination of desolation, spoken of by Daniel the prophet, stand in the holy place . . ." (Matthew 24:15).

"He [the False Prophet] exerciseth all the power of the first beast . . . doeth great wonders . . . deceiveth them that dwell on the earth by the means of those miracles . . . saying to them that . . . they should make an image to the beast. . . . And he had power to give life to the image . . . that the image of the beast should . . . speak" (Revelation 13:12-15).

Something further the False Prophet will do will be to slay all who will not worship the image, and to cause all, "both small and great, rich and poor, free and bond, to receive a mark in their right hand, or in their foreheads: and that no man might buy or sell, save he that had the mark, or the name of the beast, or the number of his name" (Revelation 13:16, 17).

There was an ancient tradition that Antichrist, when he came, would bring with him a crematorium. It would seem rather that he will be furnished with a guillotine, to judge from the number of those to be beheaded! It will include all who do not bear the mark of the beast!

"Every man," it has been truly said, "bears the marks of the master he serves." That will certainly be so during the Great Tribulation. Either they will wear the seal of the Lord or the brand of the Beast.

CHAPTER 10

The Revelation of Jesus Christ

IN HIS *Reminiscences* General Douglas MacArthur, commander in chief of the Allied forces in the Far East during World War II, related how he was compelled to evacuate the Philippines.

When his plane touched down at Batchelor Field, near Port Darwin, Australia, he was besieged by newspaper reporters, all clamoring for his comments on the situation.

He told them: "The President of the United States ordered me to break the Japanese lines and proceed from Corregidor to Australia for the purpose, as I understand it, of organizing the American offensive against Japan, a primary object of which was the relief of the Philippines. I came through, and I shall return."

The general continued in his memoirs:

"I spoke casually enough, but the phrase, 'I shall return,' seemed a promise of magic to the Filipinos. It lit a flame which became a symbol and focused the nation's indomitable will, and at whose shrine it finally attained victory. . . .

"It was scraped in the sands of the beaches. It was daubed on the *barrios*; it was stamped on the mail; it was whispered in the cloisters of the church. It became the battle cry of a great underground swell that the Japanese bayonets could not still."

The Promises

Before His withdrawal from the world the Lord Jesus registered a similar resolve. "I will come again" (John 14:3).

The parallel is not, of course, precise. In no sense whatever can the ascension of Christ rightly be spoken of as a retreat: it was a glorious upward advance. And yet there is here a striking analogy inasmuch as both promises were meant quite literally to be kept.

Of this the Bible plainly and positively and repeatedly assures us:

"Behold, the Lord cometh with ten thousands of his saints" (Jude 14).

"Immediately after the tribulation of those days . . . they shall see the Son of man coming in the clouds of heaven with power and great glory" (Matthew 24:29, 30).

"Behold he cometh with clouds; and every eye shall see him" (Revelation 1:7).

It is utterly unthinkable that it could possibly be otherwise. The last time the world saw Jesus He was skewered to a couple of wooden posts by a common highway in Israel, the execution squad of a Roman centurion standing by to make sure that the official death sentence was duly carried out.

Is it credible that that should be the final view humanity should ever get of Christ? Surely not.

At the Rapture, only "unto them that look for him shall he appear" (Hebrews 9:28). The very rapidity with which the event will take place will preclude the possibility of universal visibility. It will transpire "in a moment, in the twinkling of an eye" (1 Corinthians 15:52).

It is at the Revelation that the risen Christ will first be seen by the unbelieving race.

Where He Will Appear

At precisely what point will Christ touch down when He returns to this planet? In Scripture it is specified with the utmost geographical exactitude: "His feet shall stand in that day upon the mount of Olives, which is before Jerusalem on the east" (Zechariah 14:4). To the very locality from which our Lord ascended He will come back.

As Walter Scott reminds us, "Olivet was the last spot on earth trodden by our blessed Lord and is the first on which He stands at His return."

Accompanying Him as He decends will be not only a shining, shouting host of angels but also the saints translated at the Rapture. "The Lord Jesus shall be revealed from heaven with his mighty angels" (2 Thessalonians 1:7). "The Lord my God shall come, and all the saints with thee" (Zechariah 14:5). "The coming of our Lord Jesus Christ with all his saints" (1 Thessalonians 3:13).

As Christ's holy feet touch down in Israel, great topographical changes will take place. Here is how the prophet Zechariah describes what happens: "The mount of Olives shall cleave in the midst thereof toward the east and toward the west, and there shall be a very great valley; and half of the mountain shall remove toward the north, and half of it toward the south" (Zechariah 14:4).

Archaeologists surveying the terrain on which Jerusalem stands have stated that in that immediate vicinity there is what geologists call a "fault," a dislocation of strata or veins near the earth's surface, in which such a cleavage as that of which the Word of God speaks could occur. "Surely in that day there will be a great shaking in the land of Israel . . . the mountains shall be thrown down, and the steep places shall fall, and every wall shall fall to the ground" (Ezekiel 38:19, 20).

Every Eye Shall See Him

The Bible makes it unmistakably plain that when our Lord comes back to earth, He is going to be universally visible. "Every eye shall see him" (Revelation 1:7).

Conservative commentators have often been derided and ridiculed by liberals for believing that the Scriptures are to be taken literally when they thus predict the universal visibility of the returning Christ. When, however, in July 1969 Neil Armstrong set foot on the moon, the first man ever to do so, that miracle was almost achieved. It was officially estimated that about 600 million persons witnessed the epoch-making event.

Another suggestion as to how the returning Christ may be observed by the human population of the globe is put forward by Arthur Longley in his book *Heaven on Earth:*

"Those who cannot imagine how Christ's return to the earth is to be witnessed by the entire human race should bear in mind that it is not a momentary event but one extended through many days. He will not be earthbound when He returns, but will be manifested in glory in the heavens long enough to be seen by all. 'And then shall appear the sign of the Son of man in heaven: and then shall all the tribes of the earth mourn, and they shall see the son of man coming in the clouds . . . with power and great glory' (Matthew 24:30). This depicts a protracted, not an instantaneous event."

However the global manifestation is to take place—whether by vision or by television, instantaneously or protractedly—the Word of God declares that it will be a glorious universal demonstration of the divine majesty of Jesus. The One whom men lifted up on a Roman cross will be elevated by God above this rolling orb in power and great glory.

CHAPTER 11

The Millennium

ALMOST SINCE the dawn of civilization men have dreamed of a Millennium. They may not have called it by that name, but that is what they meant.

What *is* the Millennium? The word itself is a Latin compound comprised of *mille*, a thousand, and *annus*, year.

The term itself does not occur in Holy Scripture, but the concept is firmly planted there. In Revelation 20, within the compass of seven verses, the phrase "thousand years" appears no fewer than six times. About that there can be no question.

The question arises, How are these references to the Millennium to be construed?

Broadly, there are three views: (1) amillennialism; (2) postmillennialism; and (3) premillennialism.

Amillennialism

The expression *amillennialism* is, to be sure, a misnomer. It implies that those holding this view deny that there will be a Millennium. This is not so. What they deny is its literalness, materiality, and futurity.

According to this school of thought, the Messianic and millennial promises made by God to the Jews were fulfilled in the days of Joshua, and in the reign of Solomon, and are spiritualized in the history of the

Church. God supposedly has now finished with the Jews as a nation, and all His purposes for the ages to come are focused in the Christian society.

The mere passing of time would seem to have falsified the view which equates the Millennium with the history of the Church, since almost two millennia have gone by from its founding. Nevertheless amillennialism continues to have its eloquent advocates. But most of us feel today that we are going through the mill rather than through the Millennium!

To lend plausibility to their thesis, amillennialists interpret Scripture with the most fanciful freedom. According to William E. Cox, for example, the lion lying down with the lamb is an allegorical representation of Paul fraternizing with Barnabas!

Manifestly the divine millennial promises to the Hebrew patriarchs could not have materialized in the days of Joshua, for long after that we still see prophetic fingers pointing forward to the event as yet future. Nor can they have come to pass in the reign of Solomon because, although Solomon *did* exact tribute of kings governing countries occupying an area corresponding to that of the predicted millennial Israel, he did not himself directly govern those kingdoms. Also even in the small kingdom over which he actually did preside, the Jews did not enjoy the security of tenure unmistakably referred to in the millennial prediction: "They shall dwell in the land that I have given unto Jacob my servant, wherein your fathers have dwelt; and they shall dwell therein, even they, and their children, and their children's children for ever" (Ezekiel 37:25).

If words mean anything at all, such a divine promise as that was certainly not fulfilled in the days of either Joshua or Solomon.

Postmillennialism

Up to the close of the 19th century *postmillennialism* was the prevalent view of the Second Coming. It was widely believed that the world was gradually being Christianized—by evangelism and by legislation—and that it was only a matter of time until the Millennium would come by these means. When that happened, our Lord would return and there would be a final winding up of things.

What finally served to discredit the postmillennial position was the outbreak of the two World Wars and the constant threat of a nuclear third war.

Students of Biblical prophecy began to realize that the Kingdom cannot come until the King comes, and that in fact it is only His coming which makes its coming viable at all.

As W. Graham Scroggie cogently contends in *The Lord's Return*: "If by any process of evolution, or civilization, or promulgation of Christian principles the world could be brought into the moral and spiritual state which we associate with the idea of a Millennium, there would seem to be no need for Christ to come. What makes His return absolutely necessary, if a kingdom of righteousness is to be established on the earth, is the too obvious fact that man is utterly unable to establish such a kingdom."

If postmillennialists are right, the return of the Lord is superfluous. Christianity can conquer the world by its own inherent dynamism. Christ need not come back.

And, in any case, what is the point of His doing so if the sole purpose of His advent is to destroy the world?

We heartily endorse the sentiments expressed by George Canty in *In My Father's House*: "There are interpretations of the future and of the Bible in which

Christ is set forth as coming back merely to drop the curtain on creation. Is that a Second Coming? If there is to be no earthly reign of Jesus, no consummation of the struggle, if Christ's coming coincides with the end of the world, I may as well talk of returning to London when I only intend to drop a nuclear bomb on it."

Premillennialist

This brings us, by a process of elimination, to the last of the three classic views of the coming Kingdom—the *premillennialist*. No other fits the facts and the forecasts. This school of prophetic interpretation holds that the Bible means precisely what it says in that sometime in the future Christ will reign on this earth for a thousand years.

Let us remind ourselves of what the Bible actually does say on the subject:

"In the days of these kings shall the God of heaven set up a kingdom which shall never be destroyed" (Daniel 2:44). The implication here plainly is that, just as the 10 kingdoms are earthly kingdoms, so will Christ's kingdom be an earthly kingdom.

"In that day, saith the Lord . . . I will gather her that is driven out . . . and I will make her . . . a strong nation: and the Lord shall reign over them in mount Zion from henceforth, even for ever" (Micah 4:6, 7).

"He shall be great, and shall be called the Son of the Highest; and the Lord God shall give unto him the throne of his father David: and he shall reign over the house of Jacob for ever; and of his kingdom shall be no end" (Luke 1:32, 33).

"The kingdoms of *this world* are become the kingdoms of our Lord, and of his Christ; and he shall reign for ever and ever" (Revelation 11:15).

"I saw thrones, and they sat upon them . . . and they

lived and reigned with Christ a thousand years" (Revelation 20:4).

"Thou . . . hast redeemed us to God . . . and hast made us unto our God kings and priests: and we shall reign on the earth" (Revelation 5:9, 10).

How anyone in his senses can dispute the fact that such statements are intended to be taken with the utmost literalness is utterly inconceivable. Patently, a kingdom of a thousand years' duration on this planet, and nothing else, is here envisaged.

Where Christ bore the world's frown, He is to wear the world's crown. And the crown which is now on the false one's brow shall then belong to earth's rightful Heir.

CHAPTER 12

Marks of the Millennium

WHEN CHRIST reigns on the earth for 1,000 years—
the period we call the Millennium—what will His
kingdom be like?

Global Sovereignty

First, His rule will be over all the earth.

Daniel 2 records the mysterious dream of Nebuchad-
nezzar, king of Babylon. It was a tremendous foreview
of secular civilization.

The metallic colossus with its four metals of
diminishing value—golden, silver, brass, iron—and the
mixture of clay in its extremities was, Daniel disclosed,
symbolic of the fact that in the whole history of the race
there would be four world empires—the Babylonian,
the Medo-Persian, the Grecian, and the Roman.

The interpretation was unmistakably clear: "Thou
art this head of gold" (Daniel 2:38). The breast and
arms of silver represented "another kingdom inferior to
thee" (Daniel 2:39). Then came the thighs of
brass—apt symbol of the reproductive brilliance of
Greece. Next the legs of iron, surely an apt emblem of
the mighty Roman empire—with its two great
divisions, east and west—whose dominant characteristics were stability and mobility.

The metal image, like the human form, terminated in 10 toes. The feet were of iron mixed with clay—an incongruous combination of strength and brittleness. The 10 toes indicated a distribution of power.

"Thou sawest till that a stone was cut out without hands, which smote the image upon his feet that were of iron and clay, and brake them to pieces" (Daniel 2:34). Who is the stone? There can be no question that it is Christ who is meant.

Someone has remarked that in the Word of God the Lord Jesus is spoken of as a stone in three ways:

(1) As a *stumbling stone*. "Unto them which be disobedient, [he is] a stone of stumbling" (1 Peter 2:7, 8).

(2) As a *structural stone*. "Behold, I lay in Zion a chief corner stone" (1 Peter 2:6).

(3) As a *striking stone*. "Whosoever shall fall upon that stone shall be broken, but on whomsoever it shall fall, it will grind him to powder" (Luke 20:18).

The stone smiting the image of secular power signifies the establishment of Christ's millennial kingdom.

For the first time in history, the world is ready for global sovereignty. Radio, the telephone, television, communication satellites, and high-speed travel have made universal government a viable possibility.

Indeed, world government is being thrust upon us. The alternatives, as someone has starkly stated them, are "one world or none."

The Bible tells us that we are to have world government. Christ taught His disciples to pray: "Thy kingdom come; thy will be done in *earth*" (Matthew 6:10). Would He have prompted them to offer a petition foredoomed to frustration?

All types of government have been tried in recent times—democratic, dictatorial, autocratic, bureaucratic. One remains to be instituted—the theocratic, and all the signs are that it is about to be introduced. That will be the first mark of the Millennium—global sovereignty.

Agricultural Productivity

In passage after passage the prophets foretell that the millennial age will be one of fabulous fertility. Allowances must be made, of course, for Hebrew hyperbole, but the fact is stated so plainly that there can be no mistaking it: "Behold, the days come, saith the Lord, that the plowman shall overtake the reaper, and the treader of grapes him that soweth seed; and the mountains shall drop sweet wine" (Amos 9:13).

With the removal of the curse from nature, a large part of its potential now used in producing weeds will become valuably productive.

"Instead of the thorn shall come up the myrtle tree" (Isaiah 55:13).

"The wilderness and the solitary place shall be glad for them; and the desert shall rejoice, and blossom as the rose" (Isaiah 35:1).

Material Prosperity

The third mark will be material prosperity. This follows very naturally from what we have just said. Poverty is one of the great problems of the world today. Every time the clock ticks somebody dies because he is too poor to obtain the necessities of life.

But in Christ's kingdom it will be different. There will be a period of prodigious plenty.

"They shall build houses, and inhabit them; and they shall plant vineyards, and eat the fruit of them. They shall not build, and another inhabit; they shall not plant, and another eat: for as the days of a tree are the days of my people, and mine elect shall long enjoy the work of their hands'' (Isaiah 65:21, 22).

"They shall sit every man under his vine and under his fig tree; and none shall make them afraid'' (Micah 4:4).

Animal Tamability

Another mark of the Millennium will be animal tamability. During the Millennium the animals not only will be tamable, but they will be tame.

"The wolf also shall dwell with the lamb, and the leopard also shall lie down with the kid; and the calf and the young lion and the fatling together. . . . And the cow and the bear shall feed; their young ones shall lie down together: and the lion shall eat straw like the ox. . . . They shall not hurt nor destroy in all my holy mountain'' (Isaiah 11:6, 7, 9).

"The wolf and the lamb shall feed together, and the lion shall eat straw like the bullock: and dust shall be the serpent's meat'' (Isaiah 65:25).

For this millennial hour the whole material order is longing. "For the earnest expectation of the creature waiteth for the manifestation of the sons of God. For the creature was made subject to vanity, not willingly, but by reason of him who hath subjected the same in hope; because the creature itself also shall be delivered from the bondage of corruption into the glorious liberty of the children of God. For we know that the whole creation groaneth and travaileth in pain together until now'' (Romans 8:19-22).

During the Millennium that deep yearning will be satisfied.

Universal Tranquillity

A further mark of the millennial era will be universal tranquillity. At His first coming, Christ was introduced to the world as the "Prince of Peace" (Isaiah 9:6). At His advent was proclaimed, "On earth peace" (Luke 2:14).

When we think of the Golden Age of the future, is it not most often an era of peace we have in mind?

There is warrant for this in the Word: "He shall judge among the nations, and shall rebuke many people: and they shall beat their swords into plowshares, and their spears into pruninghooks: nation shall not lift up sword against nation, neither shall they learn war any more" (Isaiah 2:4).

As Edmund Hamilton Sears wrote:

> *For lo! the days are hast'ning on,*
> *By prophet bards foretold,*
> *When with the ever-circling years*
> *Comes round the age of gold:*
> *When peace shall over all the earth*
> *Its ancient splendors fling,*
> *And the whole world give back the song*
> *Which now the angels sing.*

Personal Longevity

An additional mark of the Millennium will be personal longevity. The normal human life-span is clearly defined by the Psalmist: "The days of our years are three score years and ten; and if by reason of strength they be fourscore years, yet is their strength labor and sorrow" (Psalm 90:10).

Modern science is doing its utmost to extend the time allotted, and it is succeeding to an extraordinary degree.

Not everybody, however, desires to lengthen the span of life. In the preface of his *Back to Methuselah*, George Bernard Shaw contended that, if the human life-span were to be lengthened to 300 years, death would be welcomed with inexpressible relief.

Doubtless that is true under present conditions. But present conditions will not be millennial conditions. Life will be desirable.

"There shall be no more thence an infant of days, nor an old man that hath not filled his days: for the child shall die an hundred years old" (Isaiah 65:20).

Ceremonial Religiosity

Yet a further mark of the Millennium will be ceremonial religiosity. I use the term *religiosity* in its better sense and imply no reflection on the quality of the worship offered by the future pilgrims to the Holy City.

By that time the Christian sacraments will, of course, have been superseded by the great events which will have transpired. Protestants acknowledge two sacraments only, both instituted by our Lord himself—baptism and the Lord's Supper. Both will have been outmoded in the millennial era. According to Matthew 28:20, baptism was to be administered until the end of this age. And in 1 Corinthians 11:26 Paul tells us that the breaking of bread is to be celebrated "till he [Christ] comes."

The Jewish sacrificial system may be reintroduced. The deduction seems warranted by such words as these: "And it shall come to pass, that every one that is left of all the nations which came against Jerusalem shall even go up from year to year to worship the King, the Lord of hosts, and to keep the feast of tabernacles" (Zechariah 14:16).

On this C. I. Scofield has an enlightening comment: "Doubtless these offerings will be memorial, looking back to the Cross, as the offerings under the old covenant were anticipatory, looking forward to the Cross. In neither case have animal sacrifices power to put away sin."

Evangelistic Activity

The final mark of the Millennium will be evangelistic activity.

There can be no contesting the fact that, according to the Word of God, the Jews are to be the great evangelists of the future. "I will send those that escape of them [the Jews] unto the nations . . . and they shall declare my glory among the Gentiles" (Isaiah 66:19).

"For if the casting away of them [the Jews] be the reconciling of the world, what will the receiving of them be, but life from the dead?" (Romans 11:15).

And so "the earth shall be full of the knowledge of the Lord, as the waters cover the sea" (Isaiah 11:9).

"If," wrote E. W. Bullinger in *Ten Sermons on the Second Coming*, "the 12 apostles and 120 disciples have sent the message of reconciliation to the uttermost parts of the earth, what will not 'all Israel' do when saved and filled with this fullness of blessing and power from on high?"

What a thrilling day it will be when, as someone has said, Christ's title of "King" will be inscribed "not as of old in three languages only but in all the tongues of the world!"

CHAPTER 13

The End of the World Is Near

RALPH WALDO EMERSON, philosopher and essayist, was approached one day by a religious fanatic who in tones of great solemnity and finality announced: "The world is coming to an end next Friday."

"Very well," answered Emerson calmly, "I can get on all right without it."

Most emphatically the world will *not* end next Friday. Much has to happen before the terminal time. The Rapture, the Great Tribulation, the Battle of Armageddon, the revelation of Christ, the acceptance of Christ as Messiah by the Jews, the millennial reign—all that is to transpire prior to what Henry Martyn termed "the final winding up of things."

Precisely how and when *will* it end? About that there are four broad views.

Some Say the World Will Not End

The first is that of those who maintain the *world is not going to end at all.* Matter, according to them, is indestructible. The universe is made of imperishable stuff. It may pass through a million permutations, but nothing of it will ever perish.

Many feel that, if this material order is going to end, its close will be so remote as to mean nothing personally to them.

They remind me of the story of the lecturer on astronomy who said to an audience: "I predict that the world will end in 70 million years." At the back of the hall a man rose in great agitation.

"Excuse me," he said, "*when* did you say the world would end?"

The lecturer, flattered by the dramatic effect his forecast had had on the hearer, replied, "I predict that the world will end in 70 million years."

The interrupter sank back into his seat with evident relief. "Oh!" he said, "thank goodness for that. I thought you said 7 million years!"

Natural Catastrophe

The second answer is that of those who predict that *the world will end as a consequence of natural catastrophe.* In accordance with their theory, they see the planet turning gradually into a huge snowball on which all life has been frozen to death, or into a burned-out cinder on which all living things have been roasted alive.

Some hold that the earth is getting bit by bit farther and farther away from the sun, its sole source of vital heat, and that the snow at present covering its polar caps will creep like white leprosy over the whole of the earth's surface.

Others maintain that our planet is slowly gravitating toward the sun and that in a few million years it will be as impossible for human beings to walk on this world as it would be for a fly to crawl on a redhot cannonball.

Thus among secular scientific prophets opinions differ sharply as to the fate of this earth, but all agree that, in any case, man has no chance of survival.

Human Action

The third answer to the question as to how the world will end is that of those who envision its *destruction as a result of human action.*

Man now has power to blow the world to bits or to wrap it in a shroud of gas or flame. Listen to H. G. Wells in *Mind at the End of Its Tether*: "The world is at the end of its rope, and the end of everything we call life is close at hand."

Or listen to Bertrand Russell. Addressing a mass rally in favor of nuclear disarmament he told the crowd bluntly that the choice before mankind is not annihilation or survival but simply for how long annihilation can be deferred.

Let's Look at the Word

The fourth answer to how the world will end is that of *the infallible Word of God.*

The Biblical view is that the end of the present world will begin at the close of Christ's millennial reign on earth.

Many people find it hard to believe that the Millennium is to conclude with a revolt. "How," they ask, "Would anyone ever wish to rebel under the benevolent rule of the Redeemer?" Surely such a state of universal tranquillity is not going to end in uproar and uprising!

That would be the natural conclusion—but there is irrefutable evidence to the contrary. Nothing is clearer in the New Testament than that the Millennium is to terminate in rebellion.

"When the thousand years are expired, Satan shall be loosed out of his prison, and shall go out to deceive the nations which are in the four quarters of the earth, Gog and Magog, to gather them together to battle: the number of whom is as the sand of the sea. And they went up on the breadth of the earth, and compassed the camp of the saints about, and the beloved city" (Revelation 20:7-9).

This will be the war to end war, the last conflict of the world. This, and not Armageddon, with which it is frequently confused, will be Satan's final fling.

Many, perhaps the majority, of those living during the Millennium will have our Lord at their *head* but not in their *hearts*. Here is proof that "the kingdom of God cometh not with observation" (Luke 17:20), but is "righteousness, and peace, and joy in the Holy Ghost" (Romans 14:17). Many who submit to the regal authority of Christ during the Millennium will doubtless do so for prudential reasons.

With the release of the devil from his thousand years' captivity, fires of revolt will be fanned into leaping flames of global war under his leadership.

The uprising, however, will be quickly quelled by heavenly incendiaries and earth's last battle be over (Revelation 20:9).

Just after this John beholds the destruction of Satan.

It is noteworthy that in the New Testament neither the devil nor his foul confederates, Antichrist and the False Prophet, are ever brought to trial. They appear before no tribunal; they are arraigned before no final judgment bar. They descend straight to destruction.

Matthew Henry's careful mind notes: "We are told that when we resist the devil, he will *flee* (James 4:7), not that he will *fall*. To destroy the devil is God's prerogative."

Universalists venture to forecast a time when even the devil will be saved. Some years ago one declared that the climax of redemption will have been reached when Jesus and Satan walk arm in arm up the golden streets of the New Jerusalem!

The Bible holds out no such hope. The devil who "sinneth from the beginning" (1 John 3:8) will go on sinning to the end. For him there is no repentance and hence no forgiveness. As Brownlow North expressed it: "The devil has gained the whole world, and lost his own soul. Who would change places with him?"

"And the devil that deceived them was cast into the lake of fire and brimstone, where the beast and the false prophet are, and shall be tormented day and night for ever and ever" (Revelation 20:10).

So will God deal a final death blow to "the god of this world" (2 Corinthians 4:4).

CHAPTER 14

The Great White Throne

THERE *IS* TO BE a last judgment. The Bible says so.

"God shall bring every work into judgment, with every secret thing, whether it be good, or whether it be evil" (Ecclesiastes 12:14).

"The Father . . . hath committed all judgment unto the Son" (John 5:22).

"God shall judge the secrets of men by Jesus Christ" (Romans 2:16).

"The Lord Jesus Christ . . . shall judge the quick and the dead at his appearing and his kingdom" (2 Timothy 4:1).

"It is appointed unto men once to die, but after this the judgment" (Hebrews 9:27).

"The Lord knoweth how . . . to reserve the unjust unto the day of judgment to be punished" (2 Peter 2:9).

"The Lord cometh with ten thousands of his saints, to execute judgment upon all" (Jude 14, 15).

"I saw a great white throne, and him that sat on it . . ." (Revelation 20:11).

Four things about the Great White Throne call for special comment. They are: (1) the Person who is the judge; (2) the people who will be judged; (3) the principles on which the judgment is meted out; and (4) the penalties that will be inflicted.

The Person Who Is to Judge

First, the *Person* who is to judge. It is supposed by some readers of the New Testament that God the Father will occupy that awful throne. But "the Father judgeth no man, but hath committed all judgment unto the Son" (John 5:22). There is eternal poetic justice in the fact that the Judge who sits on the Great White Throne will be none other than the One who once stood at the bar in Pilate's judgment hall! And what a reversal of destinies when Pilate then stands before Him!

Not as judge did Christ first come into the world. *Now* He is Saviour and Advocate. "If any man sin, we have an advocate with the Father, Jesus Christ the righteous" (1 John 2:1).

"What an Advocate!" exclaimed D. L. Moody. "He has had some hard cases to plead, but, thank God, He has never lost one!"

Jesus is to be the judge. In parable and proclamation He pictured himself in that role. "Nothing," wrote Matthew Arnold, "is more striking to me than our Lord's own description of the judgment. It is so inexpressibly forcible, coming from His very own lips, as descriptive of what He himself would do."

The People to Be Judged

Take next the *people* who are to be judged. They would seem to be classifiable into two broad groups: (1) those who rejected the preaching of Christ when He proclaimed His gospel to them in the interval between His death and resurrection (1 Peter 3:18-20); and (2) all the unregenerate dead who lived since then.

Of the first of these two groups we read in 1 Peter 4:6, "For this cause was the gospel preached also to them that are dead, that they might be judged according to men in the flesh, but live according to God in the spirit."

To the second group belong the vast mass of unregenerate mankind. "The sea gave up the dead which were in it; and death and hell delivered up the dead which were in them" (Revelation 20:13). "I saw the dead, small and great, stand before God" (Revelation 20:12).

While judgment will be universal, it will also be intensely personal. As someone has said, "God judges nations in this age, individuals in the next." That is true. And how thorough will be the scrutiny!

Men's *thoughts* will be judged. "God shall judge the secrets of men" (Romans 2:16). Men's *words* will be judged. "Every idle word that men speak, they shall give account thereof in the day of judgment" (Matthew 12:36). Men's *deeds* will be judged. "He shall reward every man according to his works" (Matthew 16:27).

Principles to Be Applied

Notice the *principles* to be applied at the Great White Throne. About the justice to be meted out three things may be said. It will be (1) impartial; (2) proportional; and (3) final.

It will be *impartial*. So often the judgments of earth are biased, either deliberately and consciously or unwittingly and unconsciously, by prejudice, ignorance, or infirmity on the part of the judge. At the Great White Throne it will not be so. "Shall not the Judge of all the earth do right?" (Genesis 18:25).

He is not prejudiced, because He loves all with equal indiscriminating affection. He is not ignorant. For "the eyes of the Lord are in every place" (Proverbs 15:3). And "all things are naked and opened unto the eyes of him with whom we have to do" (Hebrews 4:13). And

He is not infirm. "Hast thou not known? hast thou not heard, that the everlasting God, the Lord, the Creator of the ends of the earth, fainteth not, neither is weary?" (Isaiah 40:28).

The judgment of such a Judge will be incorruptibly impartial, impeccably just. There will be no bribery, no evasion of the penalty by legal technicalities, no defective evidence.

It will be *proportional*. The same sentence, carrying the same penal consequences, will not be meted out to all. In His recorded teaching our Lord makes it perfectly plain that there will be a gradation of punishments. "It shall be more tolerable for the land of Sodom in the day of judgment, than for thee" (Matthew 11:24). "That servant, which knew his lord's will, and prepared not himself, neither did according to his will, shall be beaten with many stripes. But he that knew not, and did commit things worthy of stripes, shall be beaten with few stripes" (Luke 12:47, 48).

It will be *final*. Against the verdict of heaven's high judiciary there will be no appeal. The decision will be fixed and irreversible, the judgment absolute, ultimate, and there can be neither reprieve nor release. "Every mouth [will] be stopped, and all the world . . . become guilty before God" (Romans 3:19).

Penalties to Be Inflicted

Consider the *penalties* to be inflicted at the Great White Throne. What is to be the fate of those who come up for trial at that dread tribunal? It will be too late then to pray. So far as we know from Holy Scripture, no one arraigned before that high tribunal will be acquitted. This is what our Lord himself described as "the resurrection of damnation" (John 5:29), an awful word which, although in its usages in the Word of God it does not always imply eternal loss, would seem from the context to have that meaning here. The final judgment is meted out when soul and body, copartners in crime, are at the resurrection reunited and appear before the Great White Throne.

From the judgment they are consigned to hell.

Is there a hell? Is hell simply, as Milton put it, a subjective state, or is it an objective reality? Are the pictures of it which persist in the popular mind merely bizarre relics of medieval apocalyptic?

There was a time in the history of the Christian church when hardly a sermon was heard in which there was no reference to this place of eternal retribution. Terrifying texts were quoted. "The Lord hath made all things for himself; yea, even the wicked for the day of evil" (Proverbs 16:4). That was one of them.

And fearful pictures were drawn of the fate of lost souls in the everlasting flames. Doubtless revolting figures were employed at times, but they were used for a good reason—to awaken the hearers to a sense of the reality of everlasting retribution. One would not criticize the elocution of the man whose shouts awoke one in a burning building!

One thing is certain. With the New Testament open in our hands we cannot dispute that the Lord Jesus believed in hell. Even more than He spoke of heaven He referred to that awful region, "where the tears of sorrow come too late for grace."

Consider these representative utterances:

"It is better for thee to enter into life maimed, than . . . to go into hell, into the fire that never shall be quenched" (Mark 9:43).

"Then shall he say unto them on his left hand, Depart from me, ye cursed, into everlasting fire. . . .

And these shall go away into everlasting punishment" (Matthew 25:41, 46).

"He that believeth not the Son shall not see life; but the wrath of God abideth on him" (John 3:36).

Many more passages might be quoted to similar effect. Jesus believed in hell.

Somehow guilt must be removed from the cosmos. For all who accept Christ as Saviour it was removed forever at the Cross, but so far as they are concerned who spurn the Cross, there is, as Matthew Henry said, "only one way of removing the guilt and that is by removing the guilty."

Before all who knowingly spurn the Lord Jesus stands an unimaginably awful doom. "What shall the end be of them that obey not the gospel of God?" (1 Peter 4:17).

"Oh," breaks out Wilbur Chapman, "if it be true that the *way* of transgressors be hard, what shall we say of the *end*?"

CHAPTER 15

New Heavens and a New Earth

IN OCTOBER 1938 a play, based on a novel by H. G. Wells, purporting to describe an invasion from the planet Mars, was broadcast in New Jersey. It was just before World War II. People's nerves were on edge from the international situation; and some listeners, switching on the radio after the program had begun, thought it was real. They thought the end of the world had come. Panic broke out. Telephone exchanges were jammed with frightened callers.

But if people had known their Bibles, they would have realized that the end of the world cannot come until the Rapture of the Church, the Great Tribulation, the Millennium, the General Resurrection, and the Great White Throne, have taken place.

Biblical Teaching on the End of the World

Let us see what the Bible has to say about the end of the world.

"Of old hast thou laid the foundations of the earth: and the heavens are the work of thy hands. They shall perish, but thou shalt endure; yea, all of them shall wax old like a garment; as a vesture shalt thou change them, and they shall be changed" (Psalm 102:25, 26).

"The heavens shall vanish away like smoke, and the earth shall wax old like a garment" (Isaiah 51:6).

"The former [earth] shall not be remembered, nor come into mind" (Isaiah 65:17).

"Heaven and earth shall pass away" (Mark 13:31).

"The heavens shall pass away with a great noise, and the elements shall melt with fervent heat, the earth also and the works that are therein shall be burned up" (2 Peter 3:10).

"The first heaven and the first earth were passed away" (Revelation 21:1).

What a tremendous scene! The nearest thing we know to it is a nuclear explosion. Many observers are terrified lest someone lay a fatal finger on the button that will blow the world to bits. Informed Christians know better. They recognize "the earth is the Lord's" (Psalm 24:1), and that He will not permit man to shatter it by atomic fission.

The Scriptures proclaim that the world's ultimate destiny is not destruction but reconstruction. On page after page they dwell rapturously on that thrilling theme. The Greek word *telos*, end, signifies not only cessation but consummation, not simply conclusion but completion. God will not just write "finis" but "final" to human history in order to begin a new and inconceivably wonderful chapter.

Here are the main allusions in the Word of God to this marvelous new order of things:

"Behold, I create new heavens and a new earth" (Isaiah 65:17).

"It was His loving design, centered in Christ, to give history its fulfillment by resuming everything in Him; all that is in heaven, all that is in earth, summed up in Him" (Ephesians 1:9, Knox).

"An inheritance incorruptible, and undefiled, and that fadeth not away, reserved in heaven for you" (1 Peter 1:4).

"We, according to his promise, look for new heavens and a new earth, wherein dwelleth righteousness" (2 Peter 3:13).

"And I saw a new heaven and a new earth: for the first heaven and the first earth were passed away. . . . And he that sat upon the throne said, Behold, I make all things new" (Revelation 21:1, 5).

So human history reaches its colossal climax. "Then cometh the end, when he shall have delivered up the kingdom to God, even the Father . . . that God may be all in all" (1 Corinthians 15:24, 28). Heaven will have come at last.

What Is Heaven?

Heaven will be life at its best. As to its nature the New Testament defines it by a succession of negatives—no death, no sorrow, no crying, no pain, no curse. Who would not wish to go to a place like that?

Many a saint has caught sight of it even here. Handel, describing his sensations when composing his *Messiah*, reported, "I did see the heavens open, and the Great God himself."

The seer of Revelation says, "I looked, and behold . . . a throne was set in heaven, and one sat on the throne. And he that sat was to look upon like a jasper and a sardine stone; and there was a rainbow round about the throne, in sight like unto an emerald. . . . And out of the throne proceeded lightnings and thunderings and voices: and there were seven lamps of fire burning before the throne . . . and . . . a sea of glass like unto crystal" (Revelation 4:1-6). Everything in heaven is organized around the throne.

It is this summing up of things in the divine that gives human history its value. As Harry Dean discerningly contends, "What ends in nothing is itself nothing." Nor is it otherwise with the individual human life. "Nothing short of our First Cause," observes T. H. Darlow, "will suffice for our Last End."

As to the character of the life of that blessed abode, five brief observations may here be offered:

1. *It will be spiritual.* "They shall hunger no more, neither thirst any more; neither shall the sun light on them, nor any heat" (Revelation 7:16).

"Jesus said, The children of this world marry, and are given in marriage: but they which shall be accounted worthy to obtain that world, and the resurrection from the dead, neither marry, nor are given in marriage: neither can they die any more: for they are equal unto the angels; and are the children of God, being the children of the resurrection" (Luke 20:34-36).

2. *It will be communal.* Heaven knows nothing of the hermit. "After this I beheld, and, lo, a great multitude, which no man could number, of all nations, and kindreds, and people, and tongues, stood before the throne, and before the Lamb" (Revelation 7:9).

"And I John saw the holy city, new Jerusalem, coming down from God out of heaven, prepared as a bride adorned for her husband" (Revelation 21:2).

In one of the most splendid verses ever penned William Walsham How celebrates that sublime scene:

From earth's wide bounds, from ocean's farthest coast,
Through gates of pearl streams in the countless host,
Singing to Father, Son, and Holy Ghost.
Alleluia!

Across the centuries men have looked and longed for the "city which hath foundations, whose builder and maker is God" (Hebrews 11:10). Some day we shall see it and live in its happy and harmonious community.

3. *It will be paradise*. The New Testament taxes the resources of language in trying to convey a vivid impression of its glories. Walls of jasper, gates of pearl, street of gold, a city like clear glass, sparkling like cut crystal in unfading light, a broad river bordered with richly fruited trees with healing leaves—all these are intended to produce in our minds a composite picture of a perfect environment. But the half has never been told.

4. *It will be practical.* "His servants shall serve him" (Revelation 22:3). It is indeed customary to think of heaven in terms of unending repose. Someone said, "I want to do nothing for ever and ever," but an eternal existence of that sort would be utterly unsatisfying.

Jesus told us that our Father who is in heaven "worketh" (John 5:17). Heaven puts no premium on idleness. Beyond doubt it will be a sphere of creative labor in which we shall "work for an age at a sitting and never grow tired at all."

5. *It will be eternal.* All earth's pleasures are tinged with pain by reason of their transitoriness. The full-blown rose is soon blasted. The proud prime soon passes. Summer has wings on her feet. The happiest human friendship has always hanging over it the shadow of the final parting.

In heaven it will be entirely different. There joy will not be like a taper that flickers and goes out, but rather like a star that burns on for ever. What a wonderful world it will be!

Confidently with the apostle Paul we may cry, "The Lord . . . will preserve me unto his heavenly kingdom" (2 Timothy 4:18) where "God is all in all" or as Moffatt translates it, "Everything to everybody" (1 Corinthians 15:28).